THE RISE OF BYZANTIUM

Fighting the early wars of Byzantium with *The Three Ages of Rome*

Philip Garton

The Series Editor would like to thank both Simon Clark and Nick Gaukroger for supplying photos of their figure collections.

Helion & Company Limited
Unit 8 Amherst Business Centre
Budbrooke Road
Warwick
CV34 5WE
England
Tel. 01926 499 619
Email: info@helion.co.uk
Website: www.helion.co.uk
Twitter: @helionbooks
Visit our blog: blog.helion.co.uk

Published by Helion & Company 2022
Designed and typeset by Mary Woolley, Battlefield Design (www.battlefield-design.co.uk)
Cover designed by Paul Hewitt, Battlefield Design (www.battlefield-design.co.uk)

ISBN 978-1-804510-09-4

The Rise of Byzantium

The period covered by this expansion booklet starts with the dramatic decline of the western half of the Roman Empire. Despite being the dominant force in Western Europe for more than 400 years, in less than 50 years this power was shattered and only small pockets of Roman control remained.

The following sections provide a brief guide to some of the major conflicts during the period covered by this expansion. You will see from the history below that there are many battles for you to work with during the period. The lists and scenarios included will make a good starting point for your games.

Happy gaming!

Sarmatian Heavy Cavalry (Nik Gaukroger)

The Loss of the West – the Last Battles

Early in the fifth century CE, the Roman Empire's borders were being breached increasingly by the various migrating tribes from the north and east. Some tribes became foederati (affiliated troops) for the Roman emperors and for this service they were temporarily settled within the boundaries of the Roman Empire. Their help was invaluable during a period of increasing instability. For example, the support of the Visigoths was critical in defeating the westward movement of the Huns at the battle of the Catalaunian Fields in 451 CE. It is unlikely that the Romans were very concerned by the large losses suffered by their ally.

After decades of settlement, some tribes began to expand their lands at the expense of the Empire. Two of the most important groups were the Vandals and the Visigoths. The Roman Empire struggled to contain their movements. The migrants bypassed the areas where Roman control was strongest, to settle in

Byzantine Command elements (Simon Clark)

less defended areas. At this point, it was usual for the Romans to try to push them out.

One of the longest migrations was that undertaken by the Vandals. In 330 CE Constantine the Great allowed them to settle near the River Danube in Pannonia. Then, increasing pressure from the Huns in the east caused them to migrate further west. They travelled north of the Alps and crossed the Rhine into Gaul. Around 400 CE they moved south through Gaul, across the Pyrenees and into the Iberian Peninsula. The Visigoths followed them and pushed them out of Iberia into Africa. By 430 CE the Vandals had established control over seven Roman provinces. In 435 CE, the emperor – Valentinian III – retained Carthage as part of a peace treaty with the Vandal king, Gaiseric. Less than five years later (439 CE), Gaiseric broke the peace and seized Carthage. The Vandals would rule North Africa for the next century.

That year (439 CE) was not a good one for the Romans. They tried to halt the growing power of the Visigoths and won a significant victory at the battle of Narbonne. Unfortunately, the siege of the Visigoth capital (Toulouse) was a disaster. It is said that the Roman general, Litorius, was the last significant Roman commander to observe the

ritual of the omens before a battle. They obviously did not serve him well; he was defeated, captured and died in captivity. After this battle both sides agreed to peace.

The reputation of the Roman Empire suffered a major shock in 455 CE. The navy of the Vandal King, Gaiseric, challenged Roman sea power in the Western Mediterranean. Taking advantage of the political upheaval in Rome, Gaiseric set out to raid the city. Casualties were relatively light because the emperor and his troops fled. The Vandals stayed for 14 days acquiring considerable plunder and some slaves before returning home. The situation would stabilise a little the following year when the Vandal fleet was defeated in its attempt to invade Sicily.

Elsewhere, the Visigoths were busy trying to expand their lands beyond the Pyrenees. They were successful against the Suebians (another confederation of Germanic migrants) and established themselves in the eastern coastal provinces. In 458 CE, the Romans set out to regain control over Southern Gaul. The new Roman emperor, Majorian, secured an important victory at Arelate (near Arles). The Visigoths were forced to surrender all of their territory south of the Pyrenees, to Roman control.

Byzantine Psiloi light infantry formations (Simon Clark)

When Majorian was killed by one of his own generals in 461 CE, the Roman territories in the west of Gaul split from Rome. Their leader, Aegidius, was one of Majorian's generals. He established the kingdom of Soissons. The Visigoths, led by King Theodoric II, threatened the new kingdom. Aegidius gathered support from his neighbours, the Alans and the Franks. Together, in 463 CE, they defeated the Visigoths at the battle of Orleans. The Visigoth commander Frederic, Theodoric's brother, was killed.

Three years later, Theodoric was killed by his brother Euric. Euric's rise to power would be a turning point in the history of the Visigoths. He united the various tribes under his leadership to become the first overall king of the Visigoths. In 469 CE he defeated the remaining Roman forces in Brittany at the battle of Deols. Two years later, at the battle of Arles, he achieved a crushing victory over a Roman army sent from Italy. All four Roman generals, Anthemiolus, Everdingus, Hermianus and Thorisarius, were killed. Euric advanced to reclaim Southern Gaul and the provinces south of the Pyrenees. The Romans would never recover these lands.

The migrating tribes on the Italian Peninsula added to the serious political instability in Rome. Between 455–475 CE there were eight different emperors, only one of these managed to remain in power and

rule for more than five years. During this period the power behind the throne was a Germanic general called Ricimer. In 457 CE, he helped Majorian to become emperor in the west. Majorian, however, did not bend to Ricimer's will and in 461 CE Ricimer arrested and executed him. Ricimer then established Libius Severus as Western Emperor but the Eastern Emperor, Leo, refused to recognise the appointment.

Three years later, the Alans, who had been settled as foederati in Northern Italy, rebelled against Ricimer. Their fate was decided at the battle of Bergamo. The Alan King, Beorgor, was killed and the remaining Alans were mostly absorbed by other tribal groups. Despite his successes, Ricimer did not receive any clear support from Leo. Libius Severus died in 465 CE and Ricimer governed while Rome was without an emperor.

The Vandal Gaiseric offered Olybrius as his candidate for Western Emperor. Leo rejected this, naming Anthemius as Western Emperor in 467 CE. To secure his appointment, Leo sent his Dalmatian Army to Italy as support. These troops were led by Marcellinus, who had previously fought against Ricimer. Both generals took part in an attack on the Vandal capital in Africa but the Roman fleet and the troops it was carrying, was destroyed at the battle of Cape Bon. Marcellinus was later assassinated in Sicily.

It was alleged that Ricimer had not fully supported the attack on the Vandals and in 472 CE, open warfare broke out between Anthemius and Ricimer. After five months besieging Rome, Ricimer captured and executed Anthemius, placing Olybrius on the throne. Just six weeks later, Ricimer himself died and Olybrius died four months later.

In 473 CE, Gundobad, the king of the Burgundians, with the support of the army, proclaimed Glycerius as emperor in the West, but Leo appointed Julius Nepos as emperor and forced Glycerius to abdicate. Nepos appointed Orestes as the commander of his armies. This backfired in 475 CE when Orestes installed his own son, Romulus Augustulus as emperor, forcing Nepos to flee to the east. When Leo died in 474 CE there was instability in the Eastern Empire and the new emperor, Zeno, refused to recognise Romulus' legitimacy

In 476 CE the foederati tribes of the Rugians and the Heruls, who had supported Orestes, repeated their request for more lands as their reward. Orestes refused and the foederati broke into open rebellion. The tribes proclaimed their leader, Odoacer, as king of Italy. Five days later Odoacer killed Orestes at the battle of Piacenza. He marched on to Ravenna forcing Romulus to flee. He accepted the title of king of Italy and ruled for almost 20 years until Theodoric, the leader of the Ostrogoths, killed him in 493 CE. The Ostrogoths would rule Italy for the next 60 years.

In Gaul, the last elements of Roman control were to be found in the west. Although Aegidius had defeated the Visigoths, he died just two years later. His son, Syagrius, took control of the kingdom of Soissons. He maintained good relations with the Frankish King, Childeric, and together their forces defeated a number of Saxon raids on their lands. This period of stability came to an end in 481 CE when Childeric died. His son, Clovis, aimed to unite the different Frankish tribes by acquiring the Roman territory. In 486 CE, at the battle of Soissons, Clovis defeated Syagrius and secured his kingship. He ruled for 30 years, defeating the Alemanni, the Burgundians and the Visigoths, to create the most powerful kingdom in the west.

Some Notable Battles in this Phase

458 CE – Arelate – Emperor Majorian engaged Theodoric's army near the estuary of the river Rhone. The battle was an overwhelming Roman victory. Theodoric was forced to flee and lost his kingdom. The Romans demanded the return of all Visigoth territory in Hispania.

469 CE – Deols – The Visigothic king, Euric, killed the Roman general Anthemiolus, leading to the re-capture of much of Southern Gaul.

476 CE – Ravenna – an army of rebelling foederati led by Odoacer defeated Emperor Romulus Augustulus. The Western Roman Empire collapsed and Odoacer became king of Italy.

486 CE – Soissons – Clovis, one of the leaders of the Franks, invaded the largest remaining Roman territory in Gaul. He defeated the Roman army under Syagrius and by this one battle, doubled the size of his territories. He used his success to secure his dominance over the other Frankish tribes.

Later Wars in the West – Reconquest and Defeat

Early in the fifth century the Vandals had occupied Roman North Africa. By the end of that century relations with the Eastern Empire were relatively stable until, in 530 CE, a rebellion in Sardinia forced the Vandal King, Gelimer, to send his navy and a large army to restore order. The Eastern Emperor, Justinian, saw a chance to recover some territory in North Africa. In 533 CE, a Byzantine landing in Africa under Belisarius caught the weakened defenders off guard.

Gelimer gathered his available forces and marched to meet the enemy, but at the battle of Ad Decimum, Belisarius broke the Vandal army and went on to occupy Carthage. Gelimer withdrew to await reinforcements from Sardinia. When these arrived, he tried again. The battle of Tricamarum ended in another Roman victory. Gelimer fled to the mountains and early in 534 CE he surrendered. Belisarius returned to Constantinople with the spoils of war and his prisoner in chains.

North Africa was restored to Byzantine rule, but control was limited to the main coastal areas. The local Mauri tribes had acknowledged Byzantine authority, but they soon rose in rebellion. The first imperial governor, Solomon, successfully campaigned against the tribes. He was killed at the battle of Cillium in 544 CE and the fighting continued. It was to take another 30 years until the Mauri were finally subdued.

A few years later in 552 CE, the Byzantines made a last effort to recover territory on the Iberian Peninsula by intervening in an internal struggle between rival Visigothic factions. The impact of the Byzantine intervention was decisive and they recovered the valuable territory of Baetica which contained several cities, including Malaga. This 'new' province was named Spania and it joined the Vandal and Mauri lands under the control of the Exarchate of Africa. However, the Byzantine presence irritated the Visigoths and tensions grew steadily. The Visigoths lacked the power to eject the Byzantines and it was not until 625 CE that they finally managed to push the Byzantines out of Spain.

Justinian was encouraged by his victories over the Vandals and Visigoths. On the Italian Peninsula, as in Africa and Spain, internal power struggles amongst the leaders of the Goths gave Justinian an opportunity. In March 536 CE, the Byzantine general Mundus overran Dalmatia inflicting a heavy defeat on the Goths, but he was killed in the pursuit. The Roman army withdrew, abandoning Dalmatia to the Goths. Justinian then sent Constantinianus to recover Dalmatia. Within a few months he had achieved success, the Goths withdrew to Italy and Dalmatia was back under Byzantine control.

In 538 CE, the king of the Goths, Vitiges, called for help and a large force of Burgundians crossed the Alps. Together they besieged Mediolanum (Milan), the second wealthiest city in Italy. The city

Byzantine Nikephorian Kataphraktoi (Simon Clark)

was an easy target because its defences had been neglected, it was under-garrisoned and it lacked the resources to withstand a siege. A relief force failed to help the city because disagreement between its commanders created delays that proved fatal. After months of siege, the starving garrison forced its commander to accept the Goths' terms for surrender. The garrison was released but the inhabitants were massacred and the city was devastated.

After this disaster, Belisarius was appointed overall commander in Italy and Narses joined him there. In the following year, during the campaign in the north, while the Goths and the Byzantines faced each other across the river Po, a Frankish force under Theodobert crossed the Alps and approached the Goths' camp. The Goths thought that the Franks were reinforcements but Theodobert attacked and destroyed the Gothic army! The Franks then attacked the Byzantines, who withdrew southward to Tuscany. The Franks were only stopped by a serious outbreak of disease which killed thousands and forced them to withdraw.

Belisarius concentrated on besieging the Gothic cities. Reinforced from Dalmatia, he moved against Ravenna. The King of the Goths, Vitiges, received a Frankish offer of help but, unsurprisingly, he did not trust the Franks. On the Byzantine side, Justinian offered lenient terms. He proposed

The Varangian Guard (Simon Clark)

a partition of Italy; the lands south of the Po would be retained by the Empire, those north of the river by the Goths. The Goths were ready to accept the terms and in 540 CE Belisarius entered Ravenna. The city was not looted, the Goths were well treated and allowed to keep their property. Seeing the tolerant treatment shown to Ravenna, several cities north of the Po submitted. Others, including Verona, held out. Vitiges was captured and taken to Constantinople.

Those Goths that resisted proclaimed Totila as King. To make matters worse for Justinian, a serious outbreak of plague ravaged the Empire and the Sassanids commenced a new offensive in the east. In Italy, the Byzantine commanders, Constantinianus and Alexander, failed to capture Totila's capital, Verona. In 542 CE, Totila defeated the Byzantines at the battle of Faventia and marched south towards Florence. Three different Byzantine forces marched to its relief. Totila withdrew, but surprised his pursuers at Mucellium. The Byzantines were defeated and each force withdrew to its original base.

Ten years later, in 551 CE, Narses, with a force of over 20,000 men, marched on Rome. In 552 CE, Totila tried to block Narses near to Tadinae. Totila found himself outnumbered and was forced to wait for reinforcements. When these arrived, he made his move but Narses held a strong position and the attack failed. The Goths were routed and Totila was killed. Narses went on to capture Rome and a few months later he defeated the last important Gothic army at the battle of Mons Lactarius.

With the Byzantines weakened and the Goths defeated, other Germanic tribes saw opportunities. In 553 CE, the Franks and the Alemanni crossed into Northern Italy and raided down the peninsula. In Southern Italy, the raiders split with one group aiming to return north with its plunder. This group was caught and defeated by Artabanes at the battle of Fanum. The other group pushed on as far as the Southern tip of Calabria.

Narses caught this second group as it camped on the banks of the river Volturnus, near to Casilinum in Campania. In one of his most famous battles, Narses' army virtually annihilated the raiders. Despite this success, it would take 10 more years of campaigning for the remaining areas of resistance, including the Goth capital Verona, to be returned to Byzantine control.

The effects of the plague and decades of war seriously weakened the Italian provinces. Wars against the Sassanids and along the Balkan frontier had priority with the result that the Empire largely abandoned its ambitions in the west. Within five years of Justinian's death in 565 CE, a Lombard invasion swept across Northern Italy. Expanding to occupy territories in the centre and south, the Lombards established a kingdom of Italy that would last for two centuries.

Some Notable Battles in this Phase

533 CE – Tricamarum – the Vandal king, Gelimer, reinforced by his brother Tzazon, attacked Belisarius near to Carthage. Gelimer's resistance was broken when he saw his brother killed and the Vandals were routed. The Vandal kingdom ended and their lands were added to the Byzantine Empire.

542 CE – Mucellium – having lifted the siege of Florence, the Byzantine commander, John, led the pursuit of the retreating Goths. Their King, Totila, deployed his men behind some hills to ambush John's column. The outnumbered Byzantines were broken and fled back to the main column. The sight of the advance guard routing panicked the rest of the army, which dispersed before the advancing Goths.

552 CE – Mons Lactarius – Totila was killed at the battle of Tadinae. Teia, the new king, withdrew toward Naples. He set up a defensive camp in the foothills of Mons Lactarius but Narses cut the Goths' supply line, forcing Teia to attack. Teia was killed in the fighting and the Gothic threat to Italy was effectively extinguished.

554 CE – Casilinus (Volturnus River) – Narses deployed in textbook style with an infantry centre and cavalry on each wing. His Herul foederati were some way behind his reserve. The Franks deployed in a wedge formation and charged into the Byzantine centre. They penetrated the first line but were halted by the reserve. The Byzantine cavalry moved to shoot into the Frankish flanks. The Heruls eventually arrived to join the battle. Almost surrounded, the Franks broke and fled.

Sassanid Levy Infantry (Nik Gaukroger)

The Wars in the East – Defence and Retreat

Since 440 CE relations between the eastern Roman Empire and the Sassanid Empire of Persia had been relatively stable. At the start of the sixth century this changed and after a short period of declining relations the Sassanid King, Kavadh I, ordered the invasion of the Byzantine Empire. The next four years are known as the Anastasian war. After initial successes, the Persians were pushed back by the Byzantines. Both sides lacked the resources to deliver the winning blow and the peace treaty put them back to their starting positions. The peace lasted for 20 years.

In 524 CE, the Sassanid province of Iberia (modern day Georgia) rebelled and sought Byzantine help. Two years later open warfare broke out between the Sassanids and the Byzantines. The opening phase went well for the Sassanids, they crushed the rebellion and expanded into Byzantine territory.

Sassanid Heavy Cavalry (Nik Gaukroger)

On the Syrian front, Emperor Justinian supported the Ghassanid Arabs against their enemies, the Lakhmid Arabs, who were allies of the Sassanids. In 528 CE, the Byzantine general, Belisarius, advanced into Northern Syria. He was defeated at the battle of Thannuris. Two of his generals and the king of the Ghassanids were killed. The Persians also suffered serious losses and were unable to take advantage of the Byzantine retreat.

The Byzantines resumed their offensive, winning victories at Dara and Satala. Then a serious defeat at the battle of Callinicum wiped out their earlier gains. The Byzantine court of inquiry found Belisarius responsible and he was removed from command. The Sassanid leader, Azarethes, had been unable to secure gains from his victory and Kavadh stripped him of his command. In 531 CE, Kavadh died and his place was taken by his son, Khosrow I. Justinian and the new king agreed that both sides should return to their starting positions.

The following year they signed the Eternal Peace but, as with so many other treaties, the Eternal Peace did not last. In 541 CE, the Sassanids invaded Lazica and 16 years of indecisive campaigning followed. On the Byzantine side, there was considerable political disruption between the army command and the local nobility. Two Byzantine generals murdered the local king. They were later arrested and executed. In 557 CE, both sides agreed a truce. Nothing had changed.

Justinian died in 565 CE and his nephew became Emperor Justin II. In 572 CE open warfare broke out again. The Byzantines won a victory at Sargathon but lost the stronghold of Dara. The Sassanids invaded and plundered Syria. Looking for someone to blame Justin ordered the assassination of the Ghassanid king. This plot failed and not surprisingly the Ghassanids broke off their alliance. It seems that Justin was becoming mentally unstable. His wife Sophia took charge of the Empire, supported by the leader of the Imperial Guard, Tiberius Constantine.

The new rulers restored relations with the Ghassanids. The latter then invaded Lakhmid territory and sacked its capital, Hira. In 576 CE, Khosrow made a long-range raid into Anatolia. The raid was a success but the return home was a disaster. The Sassanids were caught and severely defeated at Melitene. Khosrow sought peace but he died before any settlement was reached.

By 580 CE, the new Sassanid general in Armenia, Parviz, had recovered all the previous losses. In Mesopotamia, the new Byzantine general, Maurice, pushed into Sassanid territory and his Ghassanid allies again defeated the Lakhmids. The Sassanids under Adarmahan, counterattacked and halted the Byzantines. Maurice blamed the Ghassanids and arrested their king. The alliance once again deteriorated.

In 582 CE, Tiberius Constantine died. Maurice won a victory over Adarmahan at Constantina and was elected emperor. His general in the east, John Mystacon, was defeated by Kardarigan. The war settled into a phase of raids and talks. Victories at the battles of Solarchon and Martyropolis slowly edged the balance of power towards the Byzantines.

In the Caucasus, Byzantine and Iberian offensives were repulsed by the Persian general Bahram. He was defeated at the battle of the Araxes (589 CE) and in the traditional manner, he was dismissed by his king, Hormizd IV. With the support of his troops the humiliated general rebelled, In 590 CE, members of the Persian court killed Hormizd and proclaimed his son Khosrow II as emperor. Bahram pressed on and forced Khosrow to flee into Byzantine territory.

With support from Maurice, Khosrow set out to regain the throne. The price of this support was the restoration of Dara and several other cities to Byzantine control. In 591 CE, Khosrow and the Byzantine general Narses led an army of Byzantine and Persian troops to restore Khosrow to power. At the battle of Blarathon they killed Bahram. Khosrow handed over the agreed cities and the war came to an end. The Byzantines had finally gained an advantage in the east.

With peace in the east achieved, Maurice set off to the Balkans to deal with the Avar threat. Years of war had left the Byzantine treasury empty and Maurice's poorly paid troops mutinied several times. In 602 CE, following a major revolt, the Balkan army proclaimed Phocas as emperor and marched on Constantinople. Maurice fled but was captured and killed. Counter rebellions broke out across the Byzantine Empire.

In Mesopotamia, Narses rebelled and asked for support from Khosrow II. The latter agreed, hoping to be able to recover Armenia and Mesopotamia. The Sassanids defeated Phocas' general, Germanus, who died in battle and recovered Dara. Narses attempted a reconciliation with Phocas but he was captured and then burned alive. Phocas appointed Bonus as his leader in the east.

Massed Byzantine missile infantry (Simon Clark)

In 608 CE, the Byzantine leader in Africa, Heraclius the Elder, rebelled against Phocas and invaded Egypt. Rebellions in Palestine and Syria soon followed. Bonus dealt harshly with the Syrian revolt but failed to recover Egypt. Heraclius sent his son, Heraclius the Younger, to seize Constantinople. The Imperial Guards deserted Phocas and opened the gates of the city. Phocas was captured and executed the same day.

Taking advantage of the chaos at the heart of the Byzantine Empire, Khosrow II recovered all of his territories east of the Euphrates and in Armenia. Heraclius was unable to check the Sassanid advances. He tried to block the Sassanids at Antioch but he was seriously defeated by Shahrbaraz and the city was taken. The Sassanids advanced to Tarsus and then onto the Cilician plain, cutting the Byzantine Empire in two. Shahrbaraz captured Damascus and in 614 CE, crowned his campaign with the capture of Jerusalem. In 618 CE, Shahrbaraz invaded Egypt and within a year, Alexandria fell to him. The Byzantine Empire was on the edge of collapse.

Massed Byzantine bow armed cavalry (Simon Clark)

Heraclius' regrouped and in 624 CE he campaigned in Armenia defeating Khosrow and his generals Shahrbaraz, Shahin and Shahraplakan. In the north, the Avars joined the Sassanids, under Shahrbaraz, in the siege of Constantinople. The Byzantine defenders held out and without proper siege equipment the attack failed.

In 627 CE Heraclius resumed his offensive, defeated Rhahzadh at Nineveh and sacked Khosrow's great palace at Dastagird. Khosrow was humiliated by these disasters and was killed by his son, Kavad II. With his empire in disarray and his treasury emptied by years of war, Kavad offered to withdraw from all occupied territories. Heraclius accepted the offer and in 629 CE he triumphantly returned the True Cross to Jerusalem.

Kavad II died a few months after agreeing the peace. The various factions within the Sassanid nobility struggled to put their candidates on the throne. Kavad's seven-year-old son, Ardashir III, was proclaimed king. Then he was deposed by Shahrbaraz, whose reign lasted for three months until he was deposed by Khosrow's daughter, Boran. In turn Boran and two more candidates, were deposed. Boran was restored to the throne and managed to reign for 12 months until she was murdered.

With the Gokturk tribes raiding in the east and the Khazars attacking from the west, the factions agreed that Boran's nephew, the eight-year-old Yazdegerd III, should become king. He would become the last king of the Sassanids.

In the East – A New Power Rises

In 622 CE, far away from the wars of the Byzantines and Sassanids, an Arab leader called Mohammed established control in the city of Medina. After a series of successful battles against local tribes, his control began to grow. He died in 632 CE and his successor Abu Bakr continued the work of consolidating control over the disparate Arab tribes.

Abu Bakr died in 634 CE and was succeeded by Umar, who established the Rashidun Caliphate. It was under Umar's reign that the Arab armies exploded out of their traditional lands to confront both the Byzantine and Sassanid Empires. In less than 10 years, Umar's armies seized Syria and Egypt from the Byzantines and destroyed the Sassanid Empire.

Byzantine Thematic Kavallarioi (Simon Clark)

Umar was assassinated in 644 CE and Uthman became Caliph. He extended Arab rule over the former Sassanid territories, completing the conquest of Persia as far as Afghanistan. In the west, he resumed the wars with Byzantium by invading Armenia and continuing the advance along the North African coast.

Uthman's reign ended in 656 CE when he was assassinated by Egyptian rebels. There followed a series of leaders from the Umayyad dynasty who continued the westward drive. After 40 years of campaigning, Carthage fell to the Arabs in 698 CE. This loss marked the end of Byzantine rule in North Africa. This is an appropriate point to draw a close on Byzantium's wars in this period.

Some Notable Battles in this Phase

531 CE – Callinicum – A large force of Sassanid cavalry, led by Azarathes, raided into Syria. Belisarius's deployment was shaped by the river Euphrates. He deployed his left-wing infantry along its banks and his cavalry covered the plain in the centre. His Ghassanid allies held the right wing. Azarathes deployed his Lakhmid allies

against the Ghassanids, with his Sassanid troops on his right and centre. Early in the battle, the Lakhmids routed the Ghassanids, exposing the Byzantines' flank. The Byzantine cavalry was pushed back towards the river and eventually broke. The Sassanids could not crack the Byzantine infantry which held out. During the night it crossed the Euphrates to safety.

576 CE – Melitene – The Magister Militum Justinian caught Khosrow's army as it tried to withdraw across the river Euphrates. The disorganised Sassanids were heavily defeated. The Byzantines captured the enemy camp, including Khosrow's queen and his treasure. Returning to Constantinople with 24 elephants and thousands of prisoners, who would be sold as slaves, Justinian received his triumph from the emperor.

636 CE – Yarmuk – In Syria, the Rashidun Arab forces under al-Walid had been making good progress. The Byzantine army and its Ghassanid allies set out to stop any further losses. In a battle lasting several days, the Byzantine army was shattered. Emperor Heraclius abandoned Syria and Armenia, pulling back to create a buffer zone in Anatolia.

642 CE – Nahavand – the Rashidun Arab forces under Caliph Umar defeated the last army of the Sassanid Empire. Within ten years, the last Sassanid emperor was dead and only fragmented remains of the once great empire continued near the Caspian Sea. The resulting power vacuum would be filled with several competing factions. One of these, the Umayyads, became the dominant Arab force for the next 100 years.

Sassanid Elephants
(Nik Gaukroger)

Scenarios

Many players will simply want to recreate historical battles. The historical situation will dictate the forces and objectives for each side. We have found these games provide more interesting challenges than equal points-based games. We have provided six battles for you to consider when working on your own scenarios. There are two battles from each phase within the Rise of Byzantium.

Each scenario has a map and two orders of battle. There is also a brief history of the event to give a flavour of what to expect.

	Battle	Date	Type	Attacker		Defender
1	**Soissons**	486 CE	*Blocking*	Franks	vs	Romans
2	**Tricamarum**	533 CE	*Deliberate*	Byzantines	vs	Vandals
3	**Tadinae**	551 CE	*Blocking*	Ostrogoths	vs	Byzantines
4	**Viminacium**	599 CE	*Encounter*	Byzantines	vs	Avars
5	**Walaja**	633 CE	*Deliberate*	Arabs	vs	Sassanids
6	**Yarmuk**	636 CE	*Blocking*	Byzantines	vs	Arabs

General Notes on the Scenarios

Maps

There are few histories of the period that can provide even the most basic of battle plans. Different perspectives on the battle would lead contemporary writers to give varied accounts of the terrain and its impact on the battle. Such evidence is at best fragmentary and later writers often embellished what was known to favour particular political factions.

Orders of Battle

These reflect the historical balance of units to make up a reasoned estimate of the opposing forces. They are mostly of the 'bathtub' style (i.e. reduced ratios of strengths) to allow players the chance to create the large armies involved. Some commanders are known. Where a commander is unknown this is identified by the use of single quotation marks, e.g. 'Sigebert' at the battle of Soissons.

There is often little reliable evidence for the numbers of troops involved and even less for their training or morale. Many 'historical' accounts are unfortunately questionable. For example, following the battle of Viminacium, Simocatta wrote that over 30,000 Avars were killed and 20,000 taken as slaves. Other contemporary writers put the whole Avar strength at 20,000 mounted warriors. It is clearly difficult to ascertain any reliable figures and informed guesswork must be used.

How to read the Orders of Battle

The name(s) in bold on the first line of the box identifies a commander(s).

The following lines show the type, number of units and their training.

Example: For his command Bayan has 6 units (1 is veteran, the other 5 are trained).

Bayan		
Massed cavalry	1	V
Massed cavalry	1	T
Skirmish cavalry	3	T
Skirmish infantry	1	T

Byzantine Cataphracts (Simon Clark)

Commanders' Characteristics

There is usually little evidence about the characteristics of the majority of the lower level commanders. We suggest that you simply rate them as normal. This means that characteristics will have relatively little influence on the game.

For higher commanders there is sometimes more information. So, you may be able to agree characteristics for these individuals. If you wish to play the game without using the commanders' characteristics then simply rate all of them as normal.

Terrain Key

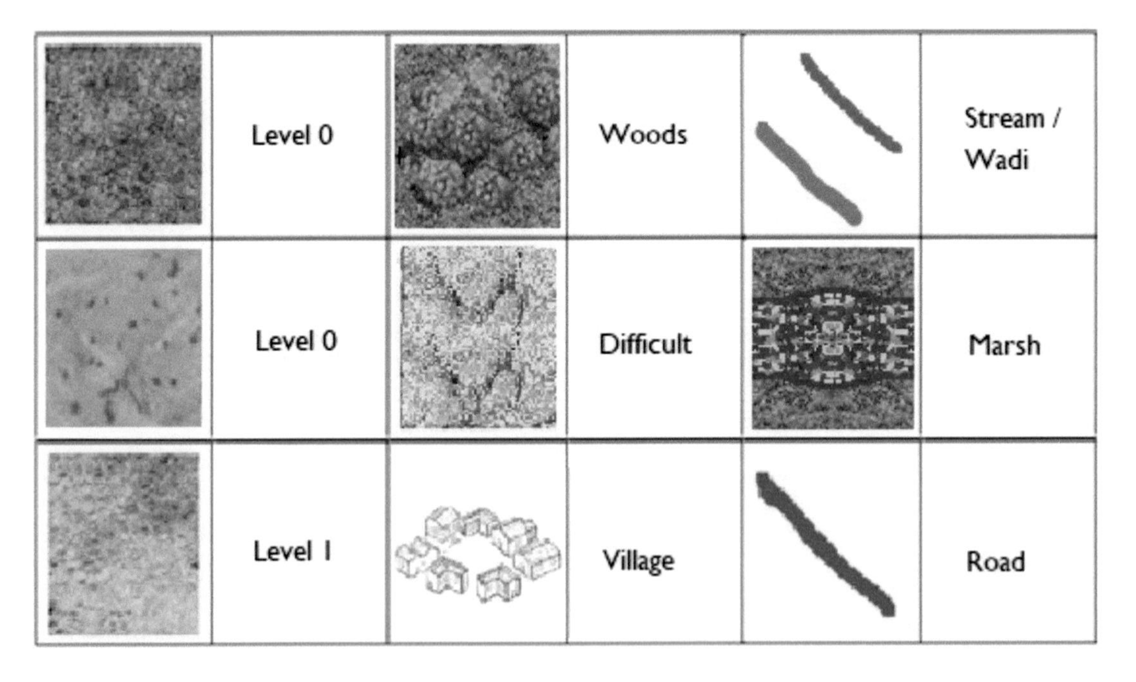

	Level 0		Woods		Stream / Wadi
	Level 0		Difficult		Marsh
	Level 1		Village		Road

The Battle of Soissons, 486 CE

During the fifth century, the western part of the Roman Empire came under increasing external pressure as various groups of Germanic tribes pushed in from the east. One of these groups was the confederation of the Frankish tribes. They passed through the lands of the Allemanni and the Burgundians, into Northeast France, eventually becoming foederati to the Romans.

By the end of the fifth century, Roman control in the west had shrunk to scattered areas. One of the most important of these was around the city of Soissons. The Franks aimed to take control of the city. It is said that the king of the Franks, Clovis, challenged the local Roman commander Syagrius to name the time and place for the deciding battle.

Syagrius had little alternative but to fight. He had to stop Clovis gaining control of Soissons. He hoped that the tensions between Clovis and some of the other Frankish chieftains would cause the Frankish army to be disrupted. Unfortunately for Syagrius, the ensuing battle was a decisive victory for Clovis. Syagrius himself fled to the neighbouring Visigoths.

It seems that Clovis considered at least one Frankish chieftain unreliable. It was alleged that Chararic stood back from the battle, possibly hoping that Clovis might be killed. Instead, after his victory, Clovis had Chararic executed as a traitor. To secure good relations with his new neighbours, the Visigothic king, Alaric II, handed Syagrius over to Clovis, who executed the Roman.

The victory secured Clovis' kingship and the realm of the Franks. They continued to enlarge their territories, eventually attacking the Visigoths, who they routed at Vouillé in 507 CE. The subsequent Frankish expansion pushed the Visigoths out of France and across the Pyrenees into Iberia. Clovis' successors continued to increase the Frankish lands and his Merovingian dynasty would rule for almost 300 years.

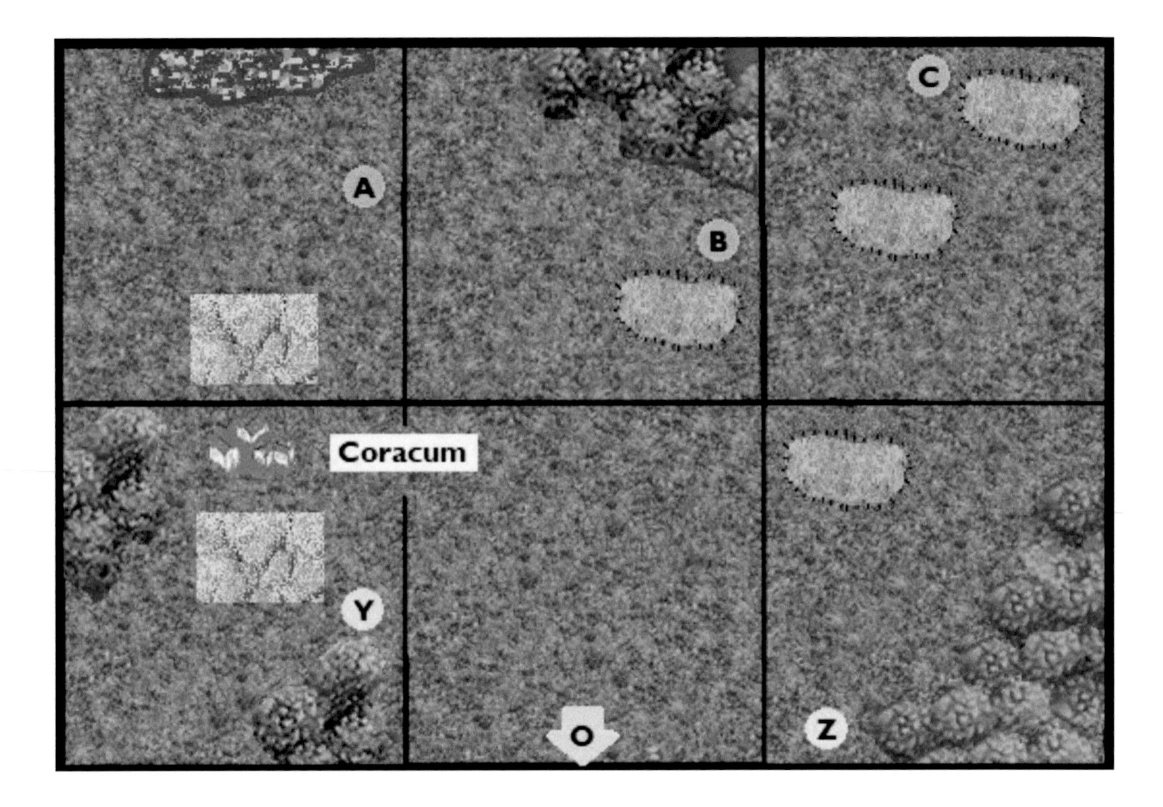

Clovis' Objective

The primary aim is to secure an exit to the south (at O). If the will of Syagrius' force is broken this route is automatically secured. This would be a victory. Any other result is a defeat. The scale of the victory/defeat is calculated using the process in Chapter 17 in the main rulebook – Victory.

Syagrius' Objective

The primary aim is to deny Clovis an exit to the south (at O). Breaking the will of Clovis' army would be a major victory.

Game time Start at 9:00 a.m. **Game length** 15 turns

Clovis and the Merovingian Frankish Army

Chararic			*'Sigebert'*			**Clovis – Army Commander**		
Massed infantry	2	T	Massed infantry	1	V	Massed cavalry	1	V
Skirmish infantry	1	T	Massed infantry	3	T	Massed cavalry	2	T
			Skirmish infantry	1	T			

Army Points and Deployment

The Franks (23 AP) deploy from the left – Clovis and Sigebert (A to B), Chararic (around C)

Syagrius' Roman Army

'Esuvian'			**Syagrius – Army Commander**			***'Lacarus'***		
Massed infantry	2	T	Massed cavalry	1	T	Massed infantry	2	T
Adaptable infantry	1	T	Skirmish cavalry	1	T	Massed infantry	1	R
Adaptable infantry	1	R				Skirmish infantry	1	T
Skirmish infantry	1	T						

Army Points and Deployment

The Romans (21 AP) deploy along Y to Z from the left – Esuvian, Lacarus, Syagrius in reserve behind Lacarus.

The Battle of Tricamarum, 533 CE

In 530 CE Gelimer deposed Hilderic to become king of the Vandals in North Africa. The majority of the nobility supported his actions. Hilderic and his supporters were imprisoned in Carthage. The governor of the Sardinian province rebelled against the usurper. Gelimer sent his brother Tzazon with 5,000 troops to crush this uprising. This weakened his forces in Africa.

The Byzantine emperor, Justinian, saw an opportunity to recover some lost territory and declared war on Gelimer. He sent an expedition, led by Belisarius, to restore Hilderic to the throne. When Gelimer heard of the Byzantine landing he ordered that Hilderic and his supporters be killed. Although their original purpose was foiled, the Byzantines continued their march on Carthage. Gelimer's weakened army blocked their way at Ad Decimum but the Byzantines were victorious. Gelimer's brother, Ammatus, was killed and the army retreated.

Four months later, Tzazon had returned from Sardinia and reinforced the Vandal army. Gelimer felt strong enough to challenge Belisarius again. This time they met at Tricamarum, about 20 miles from Carthage. Belisarius believed that his army was not strong enough to hold Carthage through the winter and decided that his best chance of winning was by a direct attack. His army closed in quickly and attacked all along the line. Slowly, the Byzantines gained the advantage and during the fighting Tzazon was killed and it has been said that the loss of a second brother caused Gelimer to lose heart. Whatever the reality, the Vandal army began to retreat, then it broke and finally it routed.

Gelimer fled to Numidia but, as the Byzantines closed in, he was forced to hide in the mountains. The next year he surrendered to Belisarius.

The Vandal rule in Africa was at an end. Their lands became part of Justinian's empire.

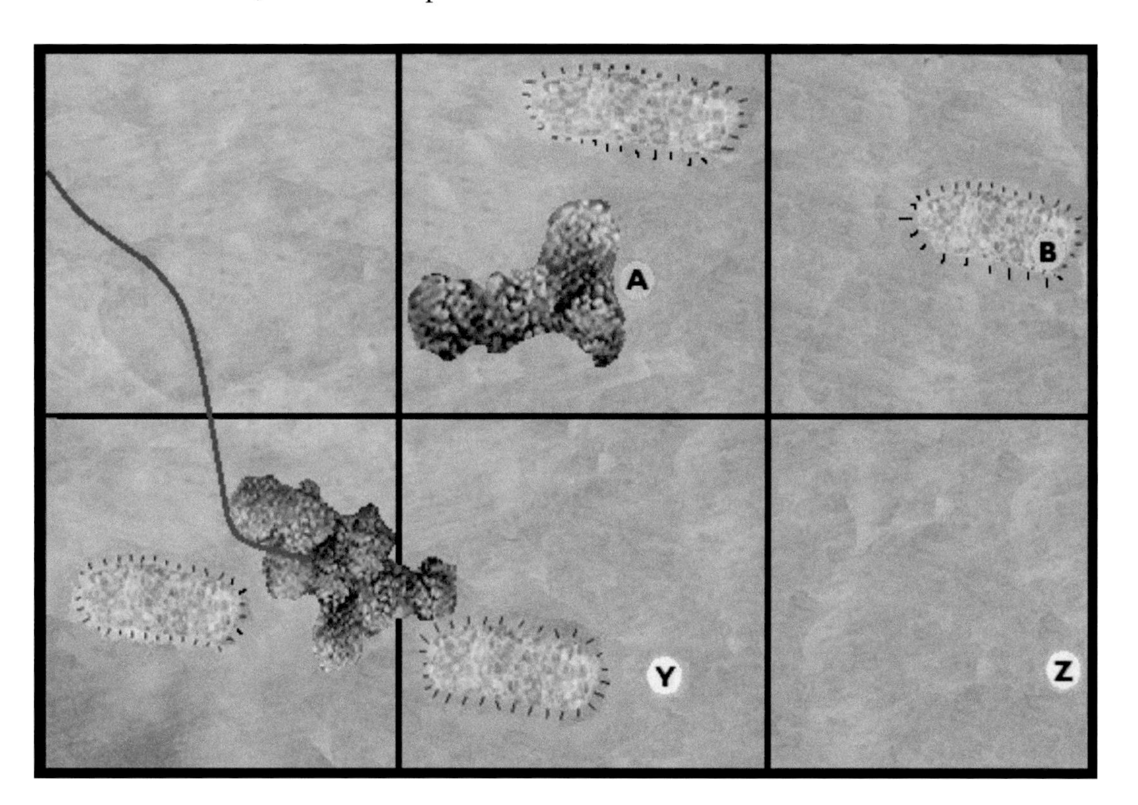

Objectives

The objective for both sides is the same.

Break the will of the enemy army and force it to retreat.

Game time Start at 10:00 a.m. **Game length** 12 turns

Belisarius' army moves first. For the first turn discard any Vandal cards up to the first Byzantine Command card.

Belisarius' Byzantine Army

'Rufinus'			*'Caisus'*			**Belisarius – Army Commander**		
Massed cavalry	2	T	Massed infantry	2	T	Massed cavalry	1	V
Skirmish cavalry	2	T	Adaptable infantry	1	T	Massed cavalry	2	T
			Skirmish infantry	2	T	Skirmish cavalry	1	T

Army Points and Deployment

The Byzantines (29 AP) deploy along Y to Z from the left – Rufinus, Belisarius.

Caisus in reserve behind Belisarius.

Byzantine Skutatoi infantry (Simon Clark)

Gelimer's Vandal Army

Gelimer - Army Commander			**Tzazon**		
Massed cavalry	2	T	Massed cavalry	2	T
Skirmish cavalry	1	T	Skirmish cavalry	1	T
Massed infantry	3	T	Massed infantry	1	T
Skirmish infantry	2	R	Skirmish infantry	2	R

Army Points and Deployment

The Vandals (28 AP) deploy along A to B from the left – Gelimer then Tzazon.

The Battle of Tadinae, 551 CE

By 495 CE the Ostrogoths had secured Italy. In 535 CE the emperor, Justinian, started a war to regain the lost territory. Within five years his general, Belisarius, had forced the Goths into submission and most of Italy was recovered. Some of the remaining Goths plotted a counter strike. One of these nobles, Totila, was proclaimed king in 441 CE and within two years he had reoccupied much of the lost territory.

Belisarius was sent back to Italy and five years of indecisive war followed. Justinian sought to end this conflict. In 551 CE, he relieved Belisarius of command and sent a large force under Narses to achieve this goal. Totila met this new threat near to the town of Tadinae. While he waited for reinforcements from other parts of Italy, he opened negotiations with Narses.

It was clear to Narses that battle was imminent so he deployed his army in a defensive position. In the centre he dismounted a large body of Germanic cavalry (Lombards and Heruls) and placed Byzantine cavalry on each flank. The Goths appear to have similarly deployed with cavalry on each wing. Initially, Totila tried a rush attack on the Byzantine left to outflank Narses' line. The attack was repulsed so he went back to his army to wait for the reinforcements.

Anticipating an attack, Narses ordered his men to have their midday meal in their positions. When the Gothic reinforcements under Teia arrived later that afternoon, Totila launched his main attack. The Byzantine army was ready and its infantry held the Gothic attack. By early evening, Narses ordered a general advance and the weakened Goths broke. At some point during this collapse Totila was killed.

The remaining Goths regrouped under Teia. Narses followed up and two years later destroyed them at Mons Lactarius. Justinian had his victory but after a decade of campaigning Italy had been ravaged. Affected by plague, the Byzantine hold on Italy was weak and short lived. By 570 CE an invasion by the Germanic Lombards had conquered most of the Byzantine lands.

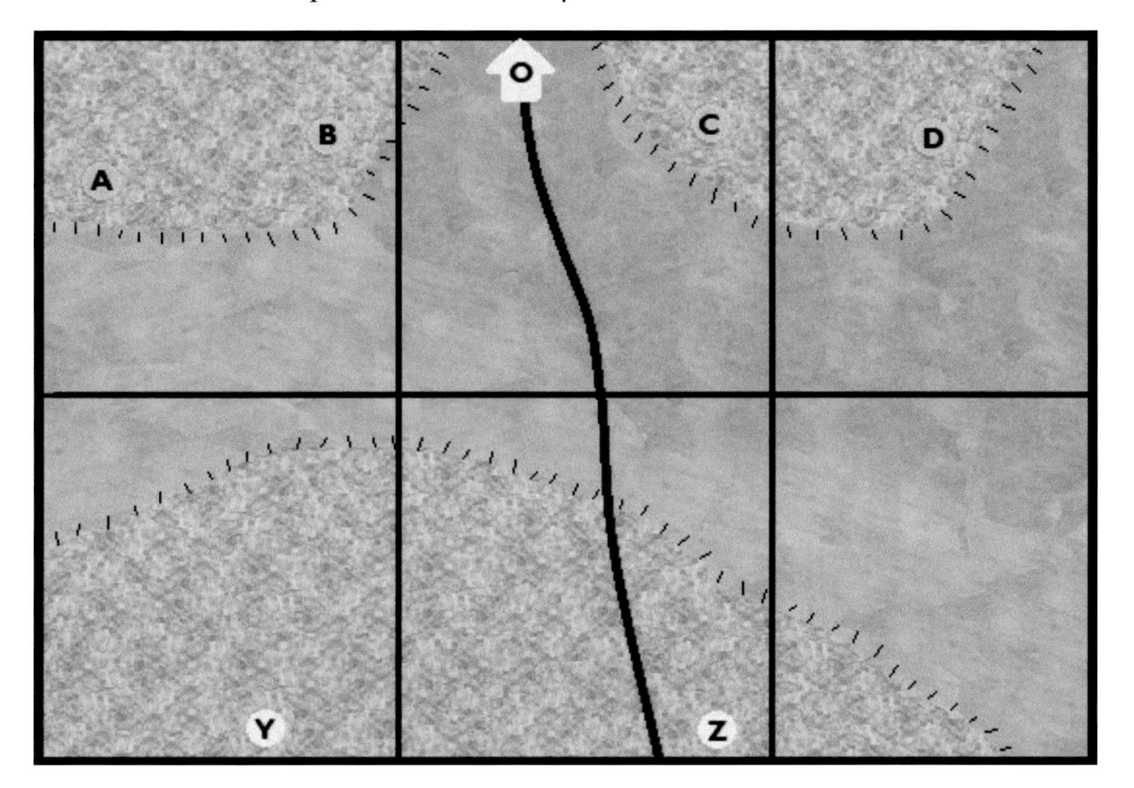

Totila's Objective

The primary aim is to secure an exit to the north (at O). If the will of Narses' force is broken this route is automatically secured. This would be a major victory. Any other result is a defeat. The scale of the victory/defeat is calculated using the process in Chapter 17 of the main rules – Victory.

Narses' Objective

The primary aim is to deny Totila an exit to the north. Breaking the will of Totila's army would be a major victory.

Game time Start at 2:00 p.m. **Game length** 12 turns

Totila's Ostrogothic Army

Teia			**Totila - Army Commander**		
Massed cavalry	2	T	Massed cavalry	1	V
Skirmish cavalry	1	T	Massed cavalry	4	T
Massed infantry	2	R	Skirmish cavalry	1	T
Skirmish infantry	2	R	Skirmish infantry	2	R

Army Points and Deployment

The Ostrogoths (33 AP) deploy along Y to Z from the left – Teia, Totila

Narses' Byzantine Army

Narses – Army Commander			**Philemuth**			**Asbadus**		
Massed cavalry	1	V	Massed infantry	4	T	Massed cavalry	4	T
Massed cavalry	3	T	Skirmish infantry	2	T	Skirmish cavalry	2	T
Adaptable infantry	1	T						

Army Points and Deployment

The Byzantines (40 AP) deploy along the line – Asbadus (A–B), Philemuth (B–C), Narses (C–D)

Byzantine Skutatoi infantry (Simon Clark)

The Battle of Viminacium, 599 CE

Around 560 CE the Avars migrated along the Northern borders of the Byzantine Empire. The emperor, Justinian, would not allow them to settle within the Byzantine lands and they moved west to the lands of the Franks. The Franks closed their borders and the Avars moved back east, into the land of the Gepids. There, allied with the Lombards, they destroyed the kingdom of the Gepids and established a homeland in the old Roman province of Pannonia. The Byzantine Empire paid the Avars to maintain a buffer zone against other 'barbarians', but payments lapsed and the Avars raided into the empire.

In 591 CE, the Byzantine emperor, Maurice, secured peace with the Sassanids and then shifted some of his veteran troops to the Balkans to halt any further advance by the Avars. In 599 CE, his generals advanced along the river Danube to Viminacium. The Avar Khagan, Bayan, had crossed the river Danube at Viminacium and invaded into Moesia. He tasked his sons with preventing the Romans from following him across the river. They failed and the Byzantines crossed the river near Viminacium.

The Byzantine general, Priscus, took the decision to go on the offensive. His advance brought the Avar army to battle near to Viminacium. This battle was a decisive success for the Byzantine general. It was suggested that the Byzantines lost just 300 men, while the Avars lost thousands. These figures are clearly questionable, but the outcome was not.

Priscus pursued the Avars back into Pannonia and was victorious in three more battles. Callinicus drove the Avar's Slav allies out of Istria and Peter defeated the Slavs in Wallachia. One contemporary Byzantine chronicler, Simocatta, says that over 30,000 Avars were killed and 20,000 taken as slaves. Several of Bayan's sons were dead and his rule was on the edge of collapse. Then, suddenly, the overthrow and death of Maurice in Constantinople provided Bayan with a lifeline. More wars would follow.

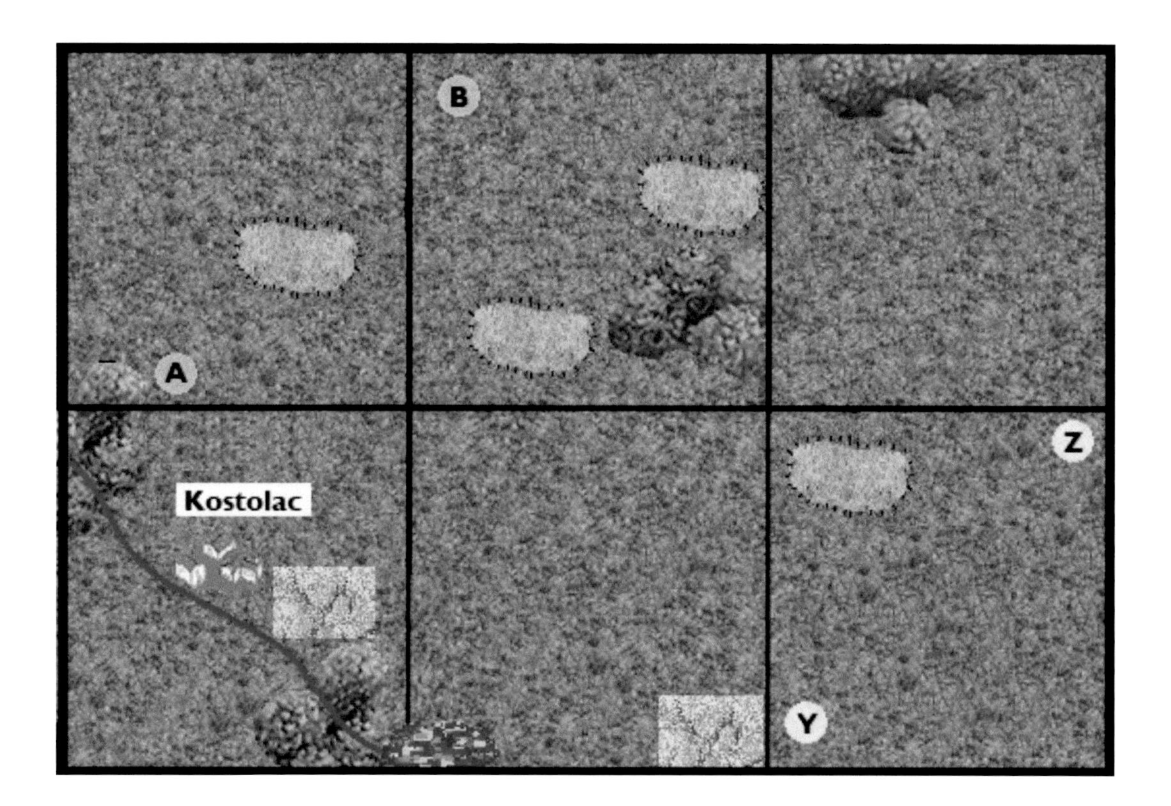

Objectives

The objective for both sides is the same.

Break the will of the enemy army and force it to retreat.

Game time Start at 10:00 a.m. **Game length** 12 turns

Priscus' Byzantine Army

'Gentzon'			**Priscus – Army Commander**			*'Padrian'*		
Massed infantry	1	V	Massed cavalry	1	V	Massed cavalry	1	V
Massed infantry	2	T	Massed cavalry	2	T	Massed cavalry	1	T
Adaptable infantry	1	T				Skirmish cavalry	1	T
Skirmish infantry	2	T				Skirmish infantry	2	T

Army Points and Deployment

The Byzantines (29 AP) deploy along Y to Z from the left – Gentzon, Priscus, Padrian.

Bayan's Avar Army

'Batbayan'			**Bayan – Army Commander**		
Massed cavalry	1	T	Massed cavalry	1	V
Skirmish cavalry	2	T	Massed cavalry	1	T
Massed infantry	2	T	Skirmish cavalry	3	T
Skirmish infantry	2	T	Skirmish infantry	1	T

Army Points and Deployment

The Avars (26 AP) deploy along A to B from the left – Batbayan, Bayan.

Germanic Tribal cavalry (Simon Clark)

The Battle of Walaja, 633 CE

The prophet Mohammed died in 632 CE and his successor, Abu Bakr, became the first Rashidun Caliph. He secured control over a large part of Arabia and began campaigning to increase the Muslim lands. The two major threats to his strategy were the established empires of the Byzantines and the Sassanid Persians. The latter was chosen as the first target because it had already been weakened by a decade of unsuccessful warfare against the Byzantines.

Abu Bakr chose Khalid ibn al-Walid to command this first campaign. The target was Hira, the capital of Sassanid Mesopotamia. After an initial victory at Kazima, the Rashidun Arab army pressed on and won a second victory at Al Madhar. The Sassanid emperor ordered Andarzaghar to take a blocking force to Walaja and wait there for a second army. Andarzaghar arrived at Walaja but the second army was late. It had set out several days later on a different route, causing a critical delay. Andarzaghar, alone and on the defensive, planned to contain the Arabs and then launch his own counterattack.

On the Arab side, al-Walid needed a victory before the second Sassanid army arrived. He organised his army and ordered a general attack. The Persian line held this first assault and Andarzaghar ordered his counterattack. The Arabs initially held but the Persian heavy cavalry slowly pushed back the Arab infantry. There was now a bulge in the Arab front line and just like the Romans at the battle of Cannae several centuries before, the Persians crowded into it.

Around this time, some detached Arab cavalry appeared over the hill behind the Persian army and charged down into its rear, causing chaos. Seizing the moment, al-Walid's flank cavalry charged in on the Persian flanks. Like the Romans at Cannae, the Sassanids were totally routed, although several thousand, including Andarzaghar, managed to escape. The victorious Arabs resumed their advance and captured Hira.

The Sassanid decline was terminal. In 636 CE, the Arabs captured the Sassanid capital at Ctesiphon. A final catastrophic defeat at Nahavand (642 CE) marked the end of Sassanid power.

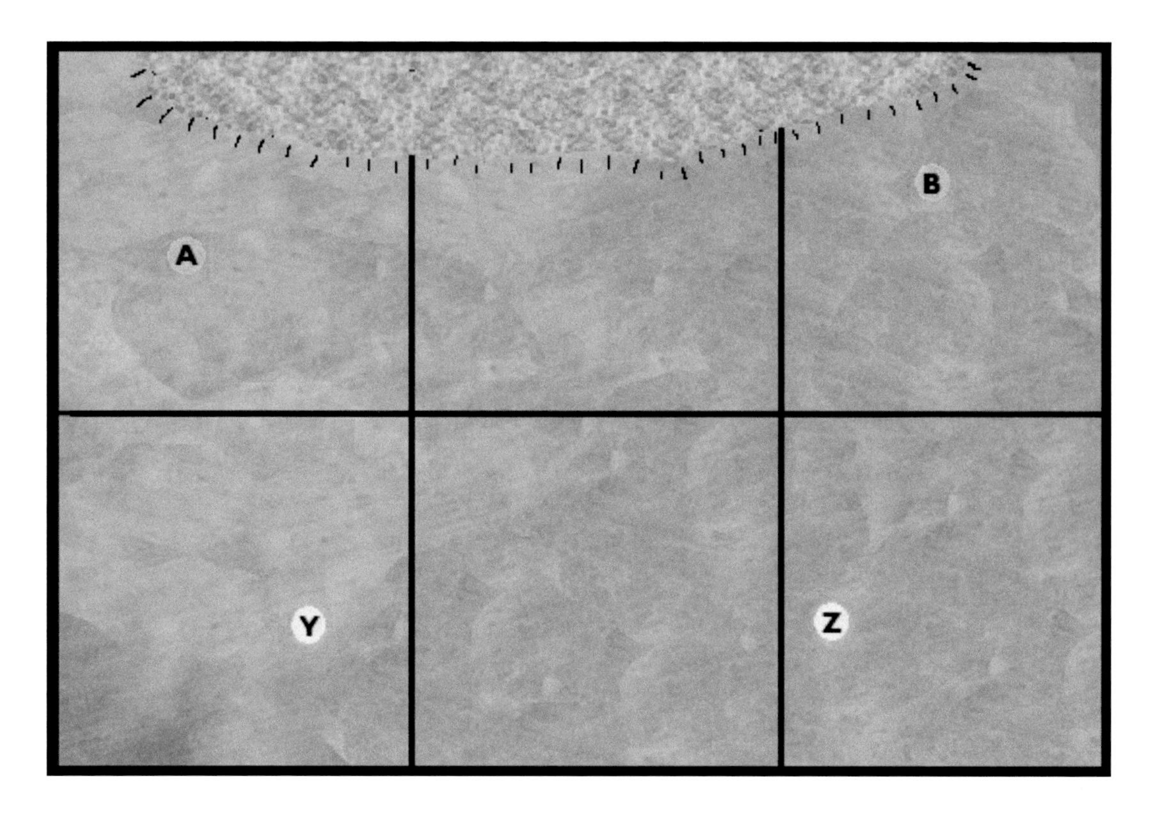

Objectives

The objective for both sides is the same.

Break the will of the enemy army and force it to retreat. Any other result is an inconclusive draw.

Game time Start at 2:00 p.m. **Game length** 15 turns

Al-Walid's army moves first

For the first turn discard any Sassanid cards up to the first Arab command card.

Special Rule

Each turn after game turn 6, when the al-Walid card is drawn, roll a D6 to see if the detached Arab cavalry appears. On a roll of 6 place a commander, Muthana, and three units of trained skirmish cavalry in the centre of the Persian table edge. At the end of the turn, place a Muthana card into the command deck. This happens only once in a game.

Al-Walid's Rashidun Arab Army

Ibn Hatim			**Al-Tamimi**			**Al-Walid – Army Commander**		
Massed infantry	1	V	Massed infantry	1	V	Massed cavalry	1	V
Massed infantry	2	T	Massed infantry	4	T	Massed cavalry	2	T
Skirmish infantry	2	T	Skirmish infantry	2	T	Skirmish cavalry	3	T

Army Points and Deployment

The Arabs (35 AP) deploy along Y to Z from the left – ibn Hatim, al-Tamimi, al-Walid in reserve anywhere behind the front line.

Byzantine Skutatoi infantry (Simon Clark)

Andarzaghar's Sassanid Army

'Al-Mundir'			*'Azadbeh'*			**Andarzaghar – Army Commander**		
Massed cavalry	2	T	Massed infantry	4	T	Massed cavalry	1	V
Skirmish cavalry	1	T	Massed infantry	2	R	Massed cavalry	2	T
Skirmish cavalry	1	R	Skirmish infantry	1	T	Skirmish cavalry	1	T
			Skirmish infantry	1	R	Skirmish cavalry	1	R

Army Points and Deployment

The Sassanids (37 AP) deploy along A to B from the left – al-Mundir, Azadbeh and Andarzaghar.

The Battle of Yarmuk, 636 CE

At the same time as his forces were destroying the Sassanid Empire, Abu Bakr's forces probed the southern provinces of the Byzantine Empire. In 635 CE the Arabs seized Damascus, then lost it to a Byzantine counterattack. Months of inconclusive manoeuvring followed. The Byzantine army was a mix of troops from the eastern field army, the Armenian field army and some Ghassanid allies. It was spread out to control the route to Damascus. The new Arab commander Khalid ibn al-Walid knew that a major battle would have to be fought for the city.

On the first day of battle, the Arabs attacked the Byzantine left flank. The Byzantines counterattacked and the Arab forces seemed to melt away. The Byzantine commander lost control as his cavalry pursued the retreating Arabs. Al-Walid was expecting this and as the Byzantines passed, he launched al-Jarrah's cavalry and his own reserve into their rear. The flanking Byzantine cavalry was routed. The isolated infantry was also routed and fled. It was said that, seeing the Byzantine flank disintegrate, the Ghassanids just melted away. The Arabs captured the left flank camp. That night, the Arabs stormed the right flank camp. The Byzantine army was now split into three isolated parts.

The following day, it became clear that the Arabs also held the vital bridge over Wadi Raqqab and that they were advancing on the left of the Byzantine centre. Outflanked on both sides, disaster loomed for the Byzantine central division. It seems that a sandstorm blew up and Vahan lost control. In the chaos, many Byzantine soldiers fled. George and Theodore died on the battlefield but Vahan may have escaped. The Arabs had orders that no prisoners were to be taken and by the end of the pursuit the Byzantine army had ceased to exist.

Al-Walid had achieved a devastating victory. The remaining Byzantine forces recoiled away. The scene was set for the Arabs to expand their conquests across Asia Minor and North Africa.

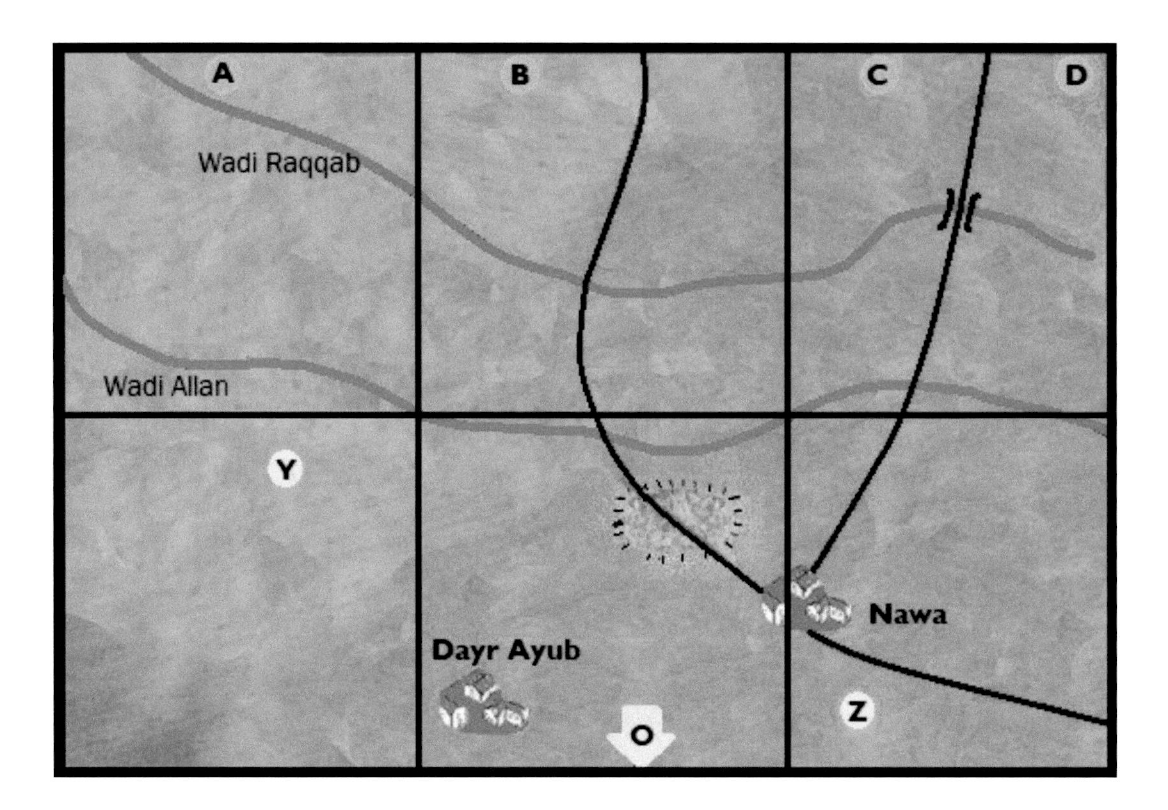

Terrain Note

The wadis were difficult going so treat them as streams. Most crossings are 'fords' except for the bridge over Wadi Raqqab.

Vahan's Objective

The primary aim is to secure a route to the Arab camp (via O). If the will of al-Walid's force is broken this route is automatically secured. This would be a major victory. Any other result is a defeat. The scale of the victory/defeat is calculated using the process in Chapter 17 of the main rules – Victory.

Al-Walid's Objective

The primary aim is to deny Vahan an exit to the south. Breaking the will of Vahan's army would be a major victory.

Game time Start at 7:00 a.m. **Game length** 18 turns

Byzantines Move First

For the first turn discard any Arab cards up to the draw of the first Byzantine Command card.

Vahan's Byzantine Army

Theodore			**Vahan – Army Commander**			**George**		
Massed cavalry	2	T	Massed cavalry	1	V	Massed cavalry	2	T
Skirmish cavalry	2	T	Massed cavalry	1	T	Skirmish cavalry	1	T
Massed infantry	2	T	Massed infantry	2	T	Massed infantry	2	T
Skirmish infantry	2	T	Adaptable infantry	2	T	Skirmish infantry	2	T

Byzantine Skutatoi infantry (Simon Clark)

Army Points and Deployment

The Byzantines (44 AP) deploy – Theodore (A–B), Vahan (B–C), George (C–D).

Al-Walid's Rashidun Arab Army

Al-Azwar			**Al-Walid – Army Commander**			**Al-Jarrah**		
Massed cavalry	1	T	Massed cavalry	1	V	Massed cavalry	1	T
Skirmish cavalry	2	T	Massed cavalry	1	T	Skirmish cavalry	1	T
Massed infantry	1	V				Massed infantry	1	V
Massed infantry	3	T				Massed infantry	3	T
Skirmish infantry	3	T				Skirmish infantry	3	T

Army Points and Deployment

The Arabs (40 AP) deploy along Y to Z from the left – al-Azwar, al-Jarrah, with al-Walid in reserve anywhere behind the front line.

Army Lists

All lists have a core worth 24 AP, plus six AP of additional units. They are intended for balanced 'game night' battles rather than historical refights.

Allies

A force may substitute six AP and a commander from one of its commands for a force of six AP and a commander drawn from the core troops of an allied army.

On rare historical occasions there were armies formed of several different allies. Where this can be shown to be the case, or if both players agree, then two commands may be substituted as above.

Note: All units have shields unless specified as shieldless.

The lists

Early Byzantines

Arab Conquest

Avars

Bulgars

Merovingian Franks

Lombards

African Vandals

The following table shows the different types of units in use throughout these rules and the abbreviations used in the various army lists. The full definitions for each type are given in Chapter 3 of the main rules.

The army points cost for each different troop type is constant throughout all of the lists, both in the core rules and the additional expansion sets, which helps when designing an individual army.

	Type	**AP cost**	**Definition**
Pb	Pike block	3 AP	p.18
HI	Massed infantry	2 AP	p.19
Ad	Adaptable infantry	2 AP	p.20
Ar	Archers	2 AP	p.21
LI	Skirmish infantry	1 AP	p.21
El	Elephants	2 AP	p.23
Art	Artillery	2 AP	p.23
HC	Massed cavalry	3 AP	p.24
Cat	Cataphracts	4 AP	A special type of Massed cavalry
LC	Skirmish cavalry	2 AP	p.25
Ch	Chariots	2 AP	p.25

Early Byzantines 450–640 CE

At the start of this period, the Byzantine army was essentially the Eastern Roman army. Over the next 200 years it fought to preserve the Eastern Empire. This list is suitable until the early seventh century when several defeats at the hands of the Rashidun Arabs led to significant reforms by the emperor, Constantine.

The Byzantine armies typically fought in two lines, with infantry in the centre and cavalry on each wing. The massed cavalry was usually armoured and carried lances. A few high-status units may have had some horse armour. It is clear that many cavalry units also carried bows and their tactics may have been similar to those of their eastern enemies. Light cavalry units were often recruited from local sources and fought in their native manner.

The massed infantry carried spears and shields. During the first 50 years of this period, they may still have carried

Hunnic Light Cavalry Archers (Nik Gaukroger)

the Roman plumbata (lead weighted darts – an impact weapon). Units that were part of the imperial field army were probably armoured, but regional troops sometimes lacked this equipment. Many infantry units included a proportion of integral supporting archers.

When there was insufficient infantry, or their units were less well-equipped, the Byzantine commanders sometimes dismounted units of massed cavalry to strengthen the infantry line. You may wish to reflect this in some of your battles, although in game terms, there is no specific difference between armoured infantry and dismounted armoured cavalry.

Commanders – Up to 4									
Core troops									
Ar	**Pb**	**HI**	**Ad**	**LI**	**El**	**Cat**	**HC**	**LC**	**Ch**
2 AP	3 AP	2 AP	2 AP	1 AP	2 AP	4 AP	3 AP	2 AP	2 AP
-	-	3	1	2	-	-	4	1	-
Additional troops – up to 6 AP from									
1	-	1	-	2	-	-	2	1	-

Notes on Troop types	
Troop Quality – Up to two units can be veteran (one HI, the other HC). Most will be trained, but a few (up to two units) can be raw (representing poorly trained, local units).	
Ar	Unarmoured, bow armed and shieldless.
HI	Up to three units of armoured spearmen. Any others would be unarmoured spearmen. Any unit may have supporting archers. Before 500 CE – up to two units may have darts (Impact weapons)
Ad	Javelin armed, unarmoured unit (probably Armenian or Isaurian hillmen).
LI	Up to two units of shieldless, unarmoured bow armed skirmishers. Any others are unarmoured with javelins.
HC	Up to one armoured unit with horse armour, armed with lance and bow.
	Up to two armoured, lance armed units. Additional units would be unarmoured. Any unit may have supporting archers.
LC	Up to two units unarmoured, shieldless and bow armed. Any others are javelin armed and unarmoured.

Arab Conquest 600–660 CE

The wars between the Byzantine and Sassanid Empires at the end of the sixth century weakened both powers. The Ghassanid Arabs fought for the Byzantines whereas the Lakhmid Arabs fought for the Sassanids. The area was full of competing tribes trying to establish dominance. In this period of turmoil, the growth of Islam dynamically changed the established patterns. This list covers the wars of the prophet Mohammed and his successors, until the establishment of the Umayyad dynasty.

Deployed Byzantine Infantry (Dan Johnson)

The infantry was usually the most numerous component of these armies. The main type was the massed unit of unarmoured, javelin-armed infantry supported by units of archers. Massed archers were sometimes used on the flanks of the infantry line.

The Arab armies usually had large numbers of unarmoured light cavalry. These were useful for raiding, scouting and skirmishing around the edges of the battle. The massed cavalry made limited use of armour and many fought unarmoured with lance and shield.

Commanders – Up to 3									
Core troops									
Ar	**Pb**	**HI**	**Ad**	**LI**	**El**	**Cat**	**HC**	**LC**	**Ch**
2 AP	3 AP	2 AP	2 AP	1 AP	2 AP	4 AP	3 AP	2 AP	2 AP
1	-	5	1	3	-	-	1	2	-
Additional troops – up to 6 AP from									
1	-	1	-	2	-	-	1	2	-

Notes on Troop types	
Troop Quality – A small number of units (up to three in total) can be veteran. Most will be trained, but some troops (up to two units) can be raw.	
Ar	Unarmoured, bow armed and shieldless.
HI	Up to one unit of armoured spearmen. The remainder are unarmoured spearmen. Any unit may have supporting archers.
	A single unit may be an unarmoured, shieldless rabble.
Ad	Unarmoured, javelin armed.
LI	Up to three units of shieldless, unarmoured bow armed skirmishers. Any others are unarmoured with javelins.
HC	Lance armed. Up to one unit of armoured cavalry. The remainder are unarmoured.
LC	Javelin armed, unarmoured.

Avars 480–630 CE

This list starts with the first serious Avar incursions into Europe. The Franks halted their westward expansion and they eventually settled south of the Danube, around the old Roman province of Pannonia. From there they raided into Italy and the Balkans. In alliance with the Lombards they destroyed the Gepid kingdom and controlled lands stretching from modern day Austria to the Northern coast of the Black Sea. Their period ends with a major civil war that led to their subjugation by the Bulgars. The remnants were finally absorbed by their various enemies during the ninth century.

Sassanid Cataphract Cavalry (Nik Gaukroger)

The Avar massed cavalry was described as carrying both lance and bow. Unusually for this period, many images show the lance being used in the ancient Sarmatian way (two-handed) and riders without shields. It also seems that, similar to the ancient Sarmatians, many horses had some frontal armour.

Commanders – Up to 3									
Core troops									
Ar	**Pb**	**HI**	**Ad**	**LI**	**El**	**Cat**	**HC**	**LC**	**Ch**
2 AP	3 AP	2 AP	2 AP	1 AP	2 AP	4 AP	3 AP	2 AP	2 AP
1	-	1	-	2	-	-	4	3	-
Additional troops – up to 6 AP from									
-	-	1	1	-	-	-	2	2	-

Notes on Troop types	
Troop Quality – Up to two units may be veteran. Most will be trained, but a few (up to two units) can be raw (representing unenthusiastic allied units).	
Ar	Unarmoured, bow armed and shieldless.
HI	Unarmoured spearmen.
Ad	Javelin armed and unarmoured.
LI	Up to two units of shieldless, unarmoured bow armed skirmishers. Any others are unarmoured with javelins.
HC	Up to two armoured, horse armour, shieldless lance and bow armed units. Up to two armoured, lance and bow armed units. Any others are javelin armed and unarmoured with shields.
LC	Up to three units unarmoured, shieldless and bow armed. Any others are javelin armed and unarmoured.

Bulgars 480–690 CE

The Bulgars were a mix of different tribes originating from the steppes of Central Asia. They were pushed westward by other migrating tribes such as the Huns and the Goths. Arriving on the edge of the Roman Empire in the late fifth century, they first served as foederati against the Goths. Around 550 CE, attacked by both the Avars and the Gokturks, the Bulgars were temporarily overwhelmed. By 580 CE they had returned and the emperor, Maurice, settled a number of the tribes in the province of Moesia, as a buffer against the Avars. Their importance would grow and in 632 CE their leader, Kubrat, established the first stages of Great Bulgaria. His legacy would last for almost 60 years.

Deployed Byzantine foot with the army high command (Dan Johnson)

This army was similar to many of the cavalry-based armies from the Eastern Steppes. They depended on their nobles to provide the massed cavalry but much of the daily work of raiding was carried out by light cavalry that were almost indistinguishable from the Huns. Infantry units were usually provided by subject tribes, sometimes willingly and sometimes not.

Commanders – Up to 3									
Core troops									
Ar	**Pb**	**HI**	**Ad**	**LI**	**El**	**Cat**	**HC**	**LC**	**Ch**
2 AP	3 AP	2 AP	2 AP	1 AP	2 AP	4 AP	3 AP	2 AP	2 AP
-	-	-	2	1	-	-	5	2	-
Additional troops – up to 6 AP from									
-	-	1	-	2	-	-	1	3	-

Notes on Troop types	
Troop Quality – Up to three units can be veteran. Most are trained, but a few (up to two units) can be raw (representing unenthusiastic allied units).	
HI	Up to one unit of unarmoured spearmen.
Ad	Javelin armed and unarmoured.
LI	Up to one unit of shieldless, unarmoured bow armed skirmishers. Any others are javelin armed and unarmoured.
HC	Up to two armoured, lance and bow armed units. Up to two unarmoured, lance and bow armed units. Any others would be lance armed and unarmoured.
LC	Up to three units unarmoured, shieldless and bow armed. Any others are javelin armed and unarmoured.

Merovingian Franks 450–750 CE

From the middle of the fifth century, the Merovingian dynasty established a dominance over the Frankish tribes that lasted for 300 years. Moving from Rome's Northern Gallic provinces, by 509 CE, they united all of the tribes under their control. They conquered most of Gaul, defeated the Visigoths, the Burgundians and the remnants of the Western Romans. Across the Rhine, many German tribes also accepted their authority. When the Western Roman Empire broke up,

Sassanid Light Infantry
(Simon Clark)

the Merovingian realm was the largest and most powerful kingdom in Western Europe.

Sometimes the noble cavalry dismounted to fight as massed infantry. To reflect this, they may be deployed as veteran massed infantry.

Commanders – Up to 3									
Core troops									
Ar	**Pb**	**HI**	**Ad**	**LI**	**El**	**Cat**	**HC**	**LC**	**Ch**
2 AP	3 AP	2 AP	2 AP	1 AP	2 AP	4 AP	3 AP	2 AP	2 AP
-	-	7	-	1	-	-	3	-	-
Additional troops – up to 6 AP from									
-	-	3	-	2	-	-	2	-	-

Notes on Troop types	
Troop Quality – Two units may be veteran. Most are trained. This army may have some raw troops (up to two units – representing less enthusiastic troops).	
HI	Up to two units of armoured spearmen. The remainder are unarmoured spearmen.
LI	Up to one unit of shieldless, unarmoured, bow armed skirmishers. The remainder are unarmoured with javelins.
HC	Up to two armoured, javelin armed units. Any additional units would be unarmoured.

Lombards 450–750 CE

The Lombards were originally from the Eastern Steppes. They had settled in the area of the Danube Basin but toward the end of the fifth century CE, the westward movement of the Avars pushed them into the old Roman province of Pannonia. From there, they provided mercenaries for a number of different Byzantine generals, including Narses. In 568 CE, seeing the weakness of the Byzantine hold on Northern Italy, they invaded. They would control this land for two centuries until they were finally defeated by the Franks.

Originally both cavalry and infantry fought with spear and shield. After contact with the Avars some of the cavalry appear to have adopted the lance. This process of change continued and by the end of the period most Lombards used the lance and shield in much the same way as their Byzantine opponents.

The infantry units were drawn from the poorer elements of Lombard society, or conscripted from the conquered territories. To give these troops to little more staying power, the cavalry could be dismounted to provide the front ranks for the infantry line.

Commanders – Up to 3									
Core troops									
Ar	**Pb**	**HI**	**Ad**	**LI**	**El**	**Cat**	**HC**	**LC**	**Ch**
2 AP	3 AP	2 AP	2 AP	1 AP	2 AP	4 AP	3 AP	2 AP	2 AP
1	-	4	-	2	-	-	4	-	-
Additional troops – up to 6 AP from									
2	-	2	-	1	-	-	2	-	-

Notes on Troop types	
Troop Quality – Up to 2 units may be veteran. Most will be trained, but a few (up to two units) can be raw (representing unenthusiastic subject units).	
Ar	Unarmoured, bow armed and shieldless.
HI	Up to one unit of armoured spearmen. The remainder are unarmoured spearmen.
LI	Up to two units of shieldless, unarmoured, bow armed skirmishers. The remainder are unarmoured with javelins.
HC	Up to two armoured, lance armed units. Up to two unarmoured, lance armed units. Any others would be javelin armed and unarmoured.

Byzantine heavy cavalry (Simon Clark)

African Vandals 400–550 CE

This list starts with the Vandals migrating south through the Iberian Peninsula and across the Straits of Gibraltar into Northern Africa. It includes Gaiseric's consolidation of the Vandals' African conquests. Perhaps their greatest achievement in this period was the capture and looting of Rome in 455 CE. For the next century, there was sporadic conflict with the Byzantine Empire. These wars continued until the famed Byzantine General, Belisarius, achieved the reconquest of the North African provinces.

It seems that the Vandal armies steadily increased their dependence on mounted troops, while the quality of their infantry suffered a corresponding decline.

Byzantine Skutatoi infantry (Simon Clark)

Commanders – Up to 3									
Core troops									
Ar	Pb	HI	Ad	LI	El	Cat	HC	LC	Ch
2 AP	3 AP	2 AP	2 AP	1 AP	2 AP	4 AP	3 AP	2 AP	2 AP
-	-	1	-	2	-	-	6	1	-
Additional troops – up to 6 AP from									
-	-	2	-	1	-	-	2	2	-

Notes on Troop types	
Troop Quality – One unit of veteran HC. Most units will be trained. This army may have some raw troops (up to three units – representing less well trained local troops).	
HI	Up to one unit of armoured spearmen. The remainder are unarmoured spearmen.
LI	Up to two units of shieldless, unarmoured, bow armed skirmishers. Any others are javelin armed and unarmoured.
HC	Up to one unit of armoured cavalry. The remainder are unarmoured. All javelin armed.
LC	Unarmoured, javelin armed.